Branding *for* Changemakers

A guide for defining and communicating your brand's impact.

DEMETRIO P. MAGUIGAD & EMILY LONIGRO

"Never doubt that a small group of thoughtful, committed citizens can change the world; indeed, it's the only thing that ever has."

MARGARET MEAD
American Cultural Anthropologist

LimeRed Studio, Inc.
4611 N Ravenswood Ave, Suite 203
Chicago, IL 60640
www.limeredstudio.com

First edition: September 2018
ISBN 978-1-7327153-0-1
Designed and written by Demetrio Maguigad and Emily Lonigro
Stock images from istockphoto.com

FOR ARETHA
- D.M. & E.L.

Contents

Why We Need Another Book on Branding

The Stakes are High.

As a business owner or entrepreneur, you've no doubt had the importance of developing a strong brand beaten into your brain. You might think: I love my logo — am I done? Answer: No.

As someone operating in the social impact space, the stakes are even higher. Branding is an essential factor to communicating your purpose and powering your mission. The time you dedicate to crafting your brand should be intentional.

"Branding" has become so nebulous that when you're developing or reinventing your messaging or visuals, you may not even know where to start. Social innovators need to take an even more nuanced approach to brand development to support their social mission. Branding is so much more than writing down some pithy statements in a Google Doc and making a cool logo. It has everything to do with how you treat people, how you communicate at scale, and how you operate your business.

So, where to get started?

We've developed this quick guide to steer you through your branding journey. It takes you step by step through some of the processes we use to define and shape our own and clients' brands over time. We map out the components that are the most important and provide tips for designing your brand while keeping your purpose and mission top of mind. We'll also show you how to leverage branding to solve business problems.

Let's do this!

CHAPTER 1

What is a Brand and Why Does it Matter?

It Must Be True.

Your brand is more impactful than
you think. If your business "does good"
then the stakes are high. In a sea of
companies who *say* they "do good,"
more and more people looking to make
a difference with where they work and
how they buy. Your decisions not only
impact your business, but others who
are attempting to do the same thing.

So if you say you "do good" and you don't
actually practice it in a meaningful way,
you're doing more damage than good.

WE LIVE IN A WORLD OF LIMITLESS OPTIONS

You're standing in the yogurt aisle at a grocery store. Should you choose plain vanilla or peach? Fruit on the bottom or not? Dannon or Yoplait? Organic or not? Which one will your kids eat? Buy three and get one free? You get the idea.

When you're stuck having to make a decision like this for the first time, it's easy to give up or just choose what is easiest. Many of us won't bother to read the ingredients, calculate price per ounce, find out where it's made, or create a spreadsheet with winners or losers to pick the perfect yogurt.

In some cases, we might pick the one closest to us, or the one that looks like it's not too generic but not too expensive. Or maybe it's the one we think has the coolest looking label. We might just go with the name that sounds most familiar.

We end up relying on our own intuition and feelings, which are influenced by how the products are positioned along the shelves, or by which images and colors we feel most attracted to. This, my friend, is branding.

STAND OUT IN A CROWD

Branding for your business is no different. You probably have a ton of competition, and you think you're different from everyone else. Are you still wondering why people see you as the same as your competition? If one of your positioning points is that you create social impact or "do good," you have a lot of work cut out for you.

A lot of companies say that and do that to varying degrees. Can we trust a brand that spills oil into the ocean because it has a green plant-based logo? Should we buy more of another brand's shoes because we know they give shoes to people in need? Who can we trust?

Branding for your business should help audiences and consumers navigate the vast number of choices presented to them. You'll need to communicate what makes you unique, show people how their values align with yours, and reassure them that they've made the right choice. And it must be true.

To accomplish this, you can do a variety of things: Choose compelling images, write a great tagline, craft impactful messaging, design a great entryway, find out what people need and help them in their lives — this is all part of your brand. When done well, all of these pieces build trust and a long-term relationship that benefits everyone.

CREATING IMPACT

When you invest in your brand, think about the impact branding has on your business performance and influence. By guiding the public perception of your business through communicating your brand, you set up the opportunity to influence behavior.

That means, you might not see change right away. Or profit. People might not get it and you might have to make changes to how you talk about what you do, or what you start the conversation with, or what you prioritize. That's OK—it's part of the process.

The idea here is to start somewhere that's true. There's no more room for overly-edited white bread marketing messages. If you operate because a system is broken and needs to change to serve humanity better, say it. Say it in everything you do — over and over and over.

People will get it. And the more of us that do this together, the faster business will be a real force for positive change.

CHAPTER 2

What is the Business Problem You are Trying to Solve?

So why do you want to develop, optimize, or redesign your brand? Typically, it's to address a business challenge or solve a problem, and you think of branding first because it's something you can see — a visual representation of the business. But creating a new logo isn't going to fix the business if there's an issue with how it runs. Luckily, branding methods can help address those underlying issues when you take them to heart.

Read the following scenarios to identify what stage you're in and what your next steps should be.

1.

Emerging or New Identity = Brand Strategy

You are just starting up your business and have been focused entirely on your model and offerings. You have yet to develop a strategy and identity to differentiate you from your competitors and communicate value as you enter the market. You need a brand strategy that will help align your business and marketing.

A brand strategy means more than having a designed logo; you need a strategic vision for how all of your written and visual assets communicate an effective and impactful identity, and an action plan for how it should be managed over time.

Ask Yourself:

What risk do I face if I keep throwing pieces out into the market without any cohesion? Do I want to keep fighting little fires? How will people choose me? What happens if they see me as the same as everyone else? How do I think the market and customers' needs will change over time?

Do:

Set a real chunk of time aside to do this work. Your business depends on how well you execute this work, so work through the models in this book, as for feedback, run customer surveys and really think about things before you send them out in the world. We entrepreneurs love shiny new projects, not usually the process, so surround yourself with people who dive deep and give great constructive feedback.

2.

Major Change = Rebrand

You're about to make a significant change in your business. It could be anything from a sudden change in leadership or a merger, resulting in a shift in priorities or vision. It could be a tweak to a fundamental service or product line the business provides. It could also be that the market or trends have changed since you began and your business needs to adapt to remain competitive and relevant.

Ask Yourself:

If I make a big change and don't tell people in a way they understand, what happens to my business? What happens if people lose faith in me?

Do:

Figure out what has been true about the business and what will continue to be true in the future. Think about what equity you have and what you want to build in the next year or two. In the Present-Future model in Chapter 7, we give you steps to do that.

3.

Disunity = Optimizing Culture

You have staff turnover issues. You find your self fighting with your vendors, clients, and employees over what you think are business fundamentals. Not everyone is committed 100% except you. No one can seem to agree on who you are, why you exist, what makes you different, or where you're going — and you have a hard time communicating that yourself. Branding methods can energize and unify your teams by creating consensus on your position, beliefs, values, and personality. When the internal team has a unified vision, communicating that to the public is a lot easier and more impactful. It's also a whole lot easier to find committed staff and vet yours vendors.

Ask Yourself:

What does my team currently believe and value about my business and does it align with my vision as a business leader?

Do:

Make sure whatever you do is inclusive and think about having someone else besides you (if you are the owner) to facilitate the process. You've probably been the decider up until now, so it will be almost impossible for you to not run the show. The models in the following chapters are ways to democratize the voices in the room, and yours needs to make way for others'.

4.

Perception Shift = Optimizing Design

You know what you do (a lot) but no one else does or they just know you for one thing. You might say, "We are an innovative business exploring concepts in data and health." But what people perceive might be, "Their ads look old and too corporate, so maybe they are a traditional pharmaceutical company." This is a perception problem. If you don't identify it or address it, this might be the thing that you will always be known for in that person's mind. Fortunately, there are some things you can do. First, you'll need to learn how people currently perceive you by capturing honest feedback. Second, figure out who you are talking to and communicate directly with them.

Ask Yourself:

What are my assumptions about my audience's perception of my brand? How might I validate these assumptions, improve perceptions, and strengthen relationships?

Do:

Listen more. You might be pushing out services or products because you have a hunch that they are what people want — and you might be right. But your ideas might have a tiny fatal flaw that will kill the whole effort. So test, test, listen, and test again before you start anything new. Consider hiring an outside company to run surveys and summarize the results so you get real results.

CHAPTER 3

Branding in Action 1: Mapping Your Audience

Before you begin working on your brand guide, you want to first understand your audience ecosystem: Who you would like to attract, who do you currently engage with, who could help tell your story, and who you can imagine interacting with your business?

REVIEW THE AUDIENCE MODEL ON THE NEXT PAGE AND FOLLOW THESE STEPS:

1. IDEATE

Think about your individual audiences — everyone your brand interacts with or wants to interact with. This could be very specific, for example, "Alice, who I met at the last show" or it can be general "art bloggers." Write them all down on Post-its or index cards.

2. ANALYZE

Take a few minutes to think through how these groups or individuals relate to one another. Can we organize them in groups with a common goal? How should we be prioritizing each of these emerging groups? Is anyone missing?

3. REWORK

Define these groups further and give them each a category name like "trade show attendees," "local media," or "business partners."

4. DEFINE

Now, consider how you might rank them. Who will help make the most impact in our mission and business? Why?

PEOPLE YOU ARE TRYING TO REACH

PEOPLE WHO CAN TELL
PARTS OF YOUR STORY

YOUR BIGGEST
FANS

PEOPLE AND ORGS
WHO KNOW ABOUT YOU
AND HAVE POTENTIAL
TO ENGAGE MORE

INDUSTRIES, MEDIA,
BIG CUSTOMER SEGMENTS

HOW TO USE THIS MODEL

Follow the steps on the previous page. First name as many audience groups as possible. Then, map them on this model. The more someone knows about your business the closer to the middle that person resides. The further out, the more work you have to do to attract their attention.

As you group the individuals, you should end up with 5-8 groups. Typically clear paths emerge from the outside to the inside.

For example, trade magazines might hit a large group of potential customers and might be a lot of work, but they are also a direct path to finding new staff and new clients for a specific service line.

This model will show you that you have a lot you CAN do and you might start to generate ideas on fun marketing projects. However, narrowing it down to what you have the capacity to execute well is tough. Rank who and what is important and start there.

CHAPTER 4

What Goes Into a Brand Guide?

Now that you have your audience mapped out, you are ready to begin creating the standards to bring consistency to your brand. Here are the branding essentials you should focus on.

BRANDING ESSENTIALS

IDENTITY ASSETS

A brand identity is a system of designed assets. The one we all think of first is the logo, but it includes all of the variations of that logo. These can include favicons, signage, cover images, social media profile images, and others.

Ask Yourself:
1. What are all of the instances in which this logo can appear?
2. How can we bring consistency to all of them so people recognize us in every medium?

BRAND GUIDE

A brand guide is set of standards for communicating the position and value of a brand to internal and external audiences. A typical brand guide includes:

Written Standards:
1. Executive Letter
2. Vision
3. Mission
4. Organization Overview
5. History
6. Name Meaning
7. Beliefs
8. Values
9. Personality
10. Tone
11. Audiences
12. Audience-Specific Messaging

Visual Standards:
1. Logo Usage
2. Color Palette
3. Photography
4. Illustration
5. Typography
6. Online Elements
7. Print Elements
8. Social Elements
9. Design Samples

Ask Yourself:
1. How might we visually communicate our brand's story in a true and meaningful way?
2. What kinds of written and visual guidance are essential for staff and contractors?
3. How might we better guide our internal and external teams to communicate our position, story, values, beliefs, and vision?

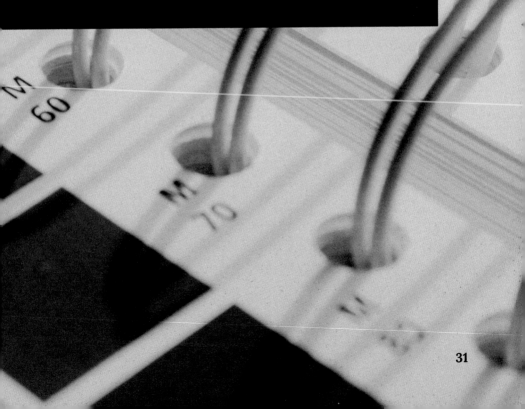

CHAPTER 5

Branding in Action 2: Developing Your Brand Voice

What does your business stand for? What keeps you coming to work every day? How do you treat people?

What is important for your business to function? What is it that you value? How should your business think, act, and present itself to the public? What is the tone in which you should speak and communicate to audiences?

All of these things are important to ask to define your brand's voice.

REVIEW THE BRAND VOICE MODEL ON THE NEXT PAGE AND FOLLOW
THESE STEPS:

1. IDEATE

Spend 1 to 2 minutes ideating your beliefs and values.
Jot down which are non-negotiables for your company or
integral parts of your mission. Spend the next 1 to 2 minutes
thinking through and writing down your personality and
tone. Are you creative, inspiring, supportive, or daring?

2. ANALYZE

Once you've mapped out these areas, spend some time
analyzing the results and discuss them with your team or
advisors. Organize the ideas so that you can form themes.
Are patterns emerging? Can you group ideas into a cohesive
narrative? Consider where you are currently and if this is
how you want to continue to be perceived.

3. REWORK

Organize the ideas so that they begin to tell your story. Do
you have a lot of single words? Groups of similar ideas? Any
outliers? Label each of these with themes, and decide, as a
group, what is true and important.

4. DEFINE

Document the emerging narrative and prioritize the ideas in
each of the brand identity areas: beliefs, values, personality,
and tone.

BELIEFS

WHAT IS TRUE?
WHY DID YOU START THIS?
WHY DOES THE WORLD NEED YOU?

VALUES

HOW DO YOU INTERACT WITH OTHERS?
HOW DO YOU TREAT PEOPLE?
WHAT MAKES PEOPLE TRUST YOU?

PERSONALITY

DOES A WELL-KNOWN PERSON EMBODY THE SPIRIT YOU'RE AFTER?
WHO IS THE BRAND IN PUBLIC AND PRIVATE?
WHAT WORDS DESCRIBE YOUR ESSENCE?

TONE

HOW DO YOU SPEAK WITH OTHERS?
WHAT QUALITIES DEFINE YOUR LANGUAGE?
WHAT QUALITIES DEFINE YOUR DELIVERY?

CHAPTER 6

Branding in Action 3: Purposeful Branding

We approach mission-driven branding through a lens of community building and company values. That process starts with uniting your internal team and existing resources.

THINGS TO CONSIDER

THE RIGHT PEOPLE

Going about these activities alone may be a bit difficult. These activities are designed to be an inclusive processes to create opportunities to ideate and gain insight with others. Consider inviting other team members, experts who are familiar with your business, and customers.

A DEDICATED FACILITATOR

The best way to approach these activities with a group is to designate a facilitator who can focus on guiding the group. The facilitator should set the tone, rules for participation, and always ensure it's a brave space for ideas — the good, the bad, but most important, the honest. The facilitator should not be an active participant, but someone who is just one step ahead of the process, always listening and synthesizing ideas, and building agreement among the participants.

DEDICATED TIME AND SPACE

Be sure to invest in dedicating time and the space to conduct these activities. Each of the activities shouldn't take longer than 60 minutes to complete. The space should be closed off from distractions (like phones).

MATERIALS

You'll need some special supplies for these activities. At LimeRed, we usually have post-it notes for ideation, thick markers to write on them so you can read from a distance, sometimes index cards to highlight important ideas. Preparing a slide deck to help guide participants through each step is also helpful.

TIMEBOXING

To maximize time and efficiency, we use timeboxing to ensure we stay on track. What is timeboxing? Timeboxing is all about putting time constraints on certain steps to help activate intuitive thinking but also to keep the session on track. One last thing to add to your materials list is a timer with an alarm. We use either a Time-Timer or even the Stopwatch app on our phones to let participants know when time is up for ideation or input.

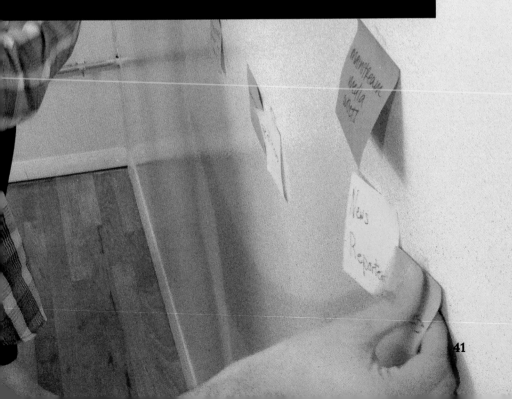

CHAPTER 7

Branding in Action 4: Present-Future Mapping

Use the next activity to think about how you might want to position your business. This activity will help you frame your business's eventual messages and value propositions by mapping out what people value and how you deliver it to them.

REVIEW THE PRESENT-FUTURE MODEL ON THE NEXT PAGE AND
FOLLOW THESE STEPS:

1. IDEATE

Take a few minutes to work with your team to brainstorm
ideas about what your audiences currently value (present)
and what you would like them to value (future) about your
business. Then, think through what you as a team value
about your business (present) and what you'd like your
team to value in the coming few years (future).

2. ANALYZE

Once you've filled in the four quadrants, spend some time
analyzing the results and discuss them with your team. Are
there patterns emerging? Do ideas overlap? Can you group
various ideas into a more cohesive narrative? Do any ideas
overlap all four quadrants?

3. REWORK

Organize the ideas so that they begin to tell a story or
narrative. Label each of these with themes if possible.
Ideally, it would be best to validate these ideas by either
conducting further research or having customers
participating in your session to confirm them.

4. DEFINE

Finally, document the emerging narrative, and prioritize the
ideas that move across each of the quadrants. Your optimal
position should cross among each of the four quadrants.

*Tip: For the best results, ask real people who are in your audiences to
participate. This could be done in person or through a survey. The Rework
and Define sections should be completed by key people in your business.*

PRESENT

HOW DO YOU DEFINE YOUR BUSINESS (GOOD AND BAD) IN THIS MOMENT?

WHAT DO STAFF, ADVISORS, AND PAST EMPLOYEES SAY ABOUT THE BUSINESS?

WHAT IS TRUE FOR EVERYONE AT ANY TIME?

WHAT DO CURRENT AND POTENTIAL CUSTOMERS SAY ABOUT THE BUSINESS?

WHAT DO OTHER STAKEHOLDERS — YOUR NEIGHBORS, VENDORS, COMMUNITY — SAY?

FUTURE

WHAT DO YOU WANT STAFF,
ADVISORS, PAST EMPLOYEES
TO SAY ABOUT THE BUSINESS?

INTERNAL VOICES

EXTERNAL VOICES

WHAT DO YOU WANT OTHER
STAKEHOLDERS — YOUR CUSTOMERS,
MEDIA, NEIGHBORS, VENDORS,
COMMUNITY — TO SAY?

Final Thoughts

1   **Know yourself.** Ensure that what you communicate aligns with your purpose, as well as what you offer by defining a brand persona and guidelines.

2   **Know your audiences** and relevant communities. Ensure that your identity communicates value and benefit that is relevant to them.

3   **Branding for your business should help** people and communities navigate the vast number of choices presented to them.

4   **Communicate what makes you unique,** help audiences understand the value you bring, and reassure them that they've made the right choice.

5   **Develop one key message** audiences can easily remember, and frame supporting messages based on audience segments.

About the Authors

EMILY LONIGRO

PRESIDENT & FOUNDER

Emily is the founder and president of LimeRed. She founded LimeRed in 2004 with a plan to prioritize high-quality design, user experience, and meaningful social impact. She has more than 14 years of experience in business, which spans design, sales, operations, user experience, branding, marketing and strategy in both online and offline programs for multinational corporations, nonprofits, universities, startups, and consumer brands.

DEMETRIO P. MAGUIGAD

PARTNER & DESIGN STRATEGY DIRECTOR

Demetrio is a partner and the design strategy director for LimeRed. He creates experiences that guide people through the complexities of today's world so that they can discover new connections, meaning, and possibilities. An expert facilitator, he brings more than 20 years of experience in design and production, research, curriculum development, storytelling, and branding.

Lime Red

ABOUT LIMERED

LimeRed is a design firm that creates social impact. Since 2004 we've built brands, businesses, and digital products that make people's lives better. And we've been doing that inclusively and deliberately, making sure all voices are heard — before that was a thing people cared about.

The world is seeking new, better, socially-conscious business practices. The current environment isn't inclusive and it's time to start doing things differently.

As a Certified B Corp and woman-owned business, LimeRed demonstrates business can be a force for good and social impact. We walk the talk, embodying and enabling progress within our team and for our clients. We are committed to mobilizing people who strive to make things better — no matter where they are in their journey. Using immersive, empathetic and structured processes, we co-create equitable, thought-provoking experiences to amplify influence and make social change.

"9 out of 10"

Thin
will n
chan

Forced
To leave

Diversity
is a
threat

If w
chang
will st
same

We are
OKAY
ON OUR
OWN

Don't
talk to
Strangers

Immigrants
are rapists,
murderers +
Stealing jobs
+ all illegal.

FUNDING
SAFE
ACTIVITP

The
will
r

not a
welcoming
city

ENGLISH
IS AN
OFFICIAL
LANGUAGE

A city
DIVIDED

Ther
too
to c
m
fan

Family
most
impor

ASSUMPTIONS

WHAT DO PEOPLE HAVE
TO BELIEVE TO ACCEPT
AS TRUTH?

67827807R00033

Made in the USA
Middletown, DE
12 September 2019